**ANCHOR BOOKS**

NATURE'S INSPIRATIONS

Edited by

Heather Killingray

First published in Great Britain in 1997 by
ANCHOR BOOKS
1-2 Wainman Road, Woodston,
Peterborough, PE2 7BU
Telephone (01733) 230761

HB ISBN 1 85930 512 1
SB ISBN 1 85930 517 2

FOREWORD

Anchor Books is a small press, established in 1992, with the aim of promoting readable poetry to as wide an audience as possible.

We hope to establish an outlet for writers of poetry who may have struggled to see their work in print.

The poems presented here have been selected from many entries. Editing proved to be a difficult task and as the Editor, the final selection was mine.

Nature's Inspirations is a collection of poems inspired by the beauty and wonders of nature.

Each poem reflects, from a personal view, the simplicity of nature, whether it be the bees collecting pollen, or a flower in bloom. Nature's Inspirations lets you experience Mother Nature and her marvels first hand; so sit back, relax and take a trip through the glorious creations of nature.

I trust this selection will delight and please the authors and all those who enjoy reading poetry.

Heather Killingray
Editor

CONTENTS

THE RED KITE

Where they on upthrust thermals ride
Nowhere but the mist to hide
A silhouette against dark clouds,
Ever moving, ever proud
Above the woodland on the hills,
Wheeling, dancing, slow until
Beneath; the winter grasses part
And some poor creature's day will start
And end, with one great swoop, a heart
Will beat no more, and pain
Will never more be felt again

Majestic bird, but do you mind
How many eyes your grace will find,
As you perform on pillowed air
For your own pleasure and not care
That you among strange landscape live
So you to others pleasure give,
The hills and vales that you survey
All handed back so we can say
For all our sins we make amends
No longer enemies, but friends

Will you feel at home and settle down
Rear your broods and spread around,
Re-inhabit land and strive
To live where once you couldn't survive,
Because in you there lies a hope
That we'll reverse the downward slope
And bring back creatures that are rare,
Back to their homes, so they can share
The joy of living, the joy of flight,
You beautiful, graceful, red winged kite.

David A Garrett

THOUGHTS ON A FROSTY MORN

So bright, so clear the fields are white
The trees stand stark and bare
And all God's World looks beautiful
A frosty nip in the air.

If I could paint the picture
Lord, I hold it in my mind
But I can only see and feel
As your love for all mankind.

I think about my selfishness
All this, all this is free.
Issues we often try to solve
Accept what has to be.

Thank you for the beauteous morn
My spirit's lifted high,
Grant all may share this inner peace,
Just once, before they die.

The sun is like a ball of fire
Canals are frozen wide
Help us to notice nature's joy,
Closed in on every side.

The hills, the fields majestic views;
I thank God, for this day
The flowers are drenched in early dew
Sure takes my breath away.

Jennifer Brazier

SNOWDROPS IN THE CHURCHYARD

A carpet of them but only bits to be seen
Just tips of white and green
Cradled in their blanket of snow
Come the sunshine and it will be a show.

Followed on by primroses and violets
Beside the road the tiny church is set
A quiet haven - only the odd footstep
To be heard along the lane.

Old folk take their little dogs for a walk
Whilst they have a talk
With only the birds to listen
And raindrops in the sunshine glisten.

Myrtle E Holmes

A YEAR

Winter is over we now turn to spring
The trees are budding the birds start to sing,
With bulbs all peeping through the ground,
It makes life happy to be around,
Now is the time to buy all the seeds,
For the fruit and flowers the summer time needs,
We have to have sun and also the rain
To help the flowers to bloom again,
The children love the long summer days,
To go to the park where all children play.
Then comes the autumn and the leaves fall.
It comes as a reminder to us all,
That winter approaches once more again,
So we expect the snow and the rain
Happy to know spring will come round for sure,
And everything will repeat over once more.

J Willson

LATE WINTER DAYS

The beauty of earth, on a winter day,
Faint stirrings of living things.
A small fresh breeze blows mists away,
Spring's sweetness on its wings.

New violet leaves, in cold wet soil,
New stirrings in the earth,
And tiny spears that upward toil,
Our blessèd earth's re-birth.

Pink streaked skies in the evening light
A great hope in the land,
And joy that I still live, and might,
Hold beauty in my hands.

M J Fisher

THE PROMISE

Look, - see how the hedgerows, - sombre brown
Turn gentle green, now spring bestrides the land,
All hedge and hill, vale and down
Breaks free again from winter's hand.

Each year this promise, fresh renewed
Brings forth the signs of life's rebirth,
All mankind awaits, - all fears subdued
When spring holds court, in this dear land.

H E Hayward

ABOVE ALL

Look around please and tell us what you see.
All that grows and breathes are signposts for me.
Each life has its own way pre-ordained
From earliest days, to a time as arranged.
As naturally as a seed shoots tall
All that happens is written on the wall.
We can help in a way as up they grow
Keeping them ready for a spring-time show.
You have a place in the order of things.
When you learn this is true it puts a spring
In your step, with company you know you'll keep.
The rewards are sweet in the dreams they'll reap.
Whatever your beliefs the road is clear,
Above all it's Nature which we hold dear.

Hugh Lincoln

THE WIND

The wind was howling round the house
where I lay, quiet as a mouse,
the windows rattled and into battle
marched the soldiers on the panes.

The wildness of the night
was a frightening sight
the clouds rushing across the sky
gathering to attack from on high

The 'heavens' were so black and angry
as the wind howled and whistled
through every nook and cranny
making the room feel chill and bristled.

Then suddenly, its fury spent
no more its anger to vent
just a rustling in the trees
it whispered, 'you're safe with me.'

Sally Salisbury

A THING OF BEAUTY

I never took much notice of a tree,
Until the 'flu virus took a hold on me.
I could not leave the house,
All I did was grouse.

Then one morning I looked at the trees,
I suddenly saw beauty standing there
Overnight snow had fallen, covering everything in sight,
The trees were covered with lace of pure white.
I could not take my eyes from the scene,
The day before their leaves were peeping green
Now branches were bent to the ground, it saddened me to see
                                                    proud trees,
Looking so forlorn, brought to their knees,
Then suddenly the thaw started, I watched the boughs
                                                    gradually fall apart.
Soon they were once again standing proud,
The branches reaching upwards to the clouds.
Now I am waiting for spring to come,
To see the trees with new shoots of life,
Reach out their arms to the sun.
Never again can I take trees for granted,
I'm so thrilled to know that trees will always be planted.

W Hart

MY PERSIAN CAT

When I was a little girl,
I had a Persian cat.
I cuddled him and loved him
This he knew.

Then one day there was a show,
For cats and dogs and rabbits.
I thought I'd put my Persian
Cat in for the show.

He was big and beautiful,
In every way.
The next-door lady, she did not like him
So she put poison on the wall.

A day before the show was due,
He died a tragic death,
I'm now much older in my prime.
But I will never let him go.

My big beautiful Persian cat.

Jean Rickwood

TAIR ONEN

Coniferous fragrance fills the breeze, rustling fronds
Murmur in seed-blown air, some fallen bark alive
With life, flattens the fire-flowers bare.
Around the lake, the rushes sharp, point arrowed swords
Towards the sky and cotton grass with silky hair a
Blanket does endow on murky water, lapping onwards
Disturbed by rings of breath of fish, who for
Clean air break through, from muddy hidden lair.

Green acrobatic frogs, in thousands leap the edge
Their limbs enact a grotesque jig and passing
Insects swarm above, frantic to avoid their yawn.
Gangling legs and bulging eyes, collision in mid-
Stream abounds, whilst jellied eggs of bubbled mass
Silently move around. The earth is spongy, slimed by
Weed; mosaic cracked away from bank. Scarlet
Pimpernel struggles here, nestling in the rifts.

As you look towards those clouds, a creaking twig
Will tell, a hungry squirrel cracking nuts, his tail
Braked around a branch, watches carefully the scene
Below. he nibbles as he stares and bramble thorns
With piercing pins, clamber to protect his leafy home.
Soon rain will form and plants will sup, this moisture
Cool and pure and Tair Onen's 'cup will overflow'
In Nature's rapturous fare.

Joan Richardson

AS I GAZE FROM MY WINDOW

As I gaze from my window,
I see a wondrous sight,
The fields are white and dazzling,
It must have snowed all night.
Suddenly the sun breaks through,
The snow begins to melt
The earth is getting greener now
A new warmth now is felt
The spring has come
The birds awake
The early-morning chorus
Just makes us glad to be alive
With all that is going for us
Then summer, now, that lovely season
With all its joy and pleasure
Day of sunshine, nights of joy
And memories to treasure
Autumn comes, a blaze of gold
The year is fading fast
With winter here I have no fear
My happiness will last.

L Sonart

SUMMER'S SONG

How wonderful, how truly fine
That summer comes with breath like wine
And with her travels the gentle breeze
To whisper through the grass and trees
And thus caress the sleeping rose
To waken her from sweet repose.
Her perfume drifting on the dawn
To linger on in warmth of morn.
And every fleecy cloud so white
Will add to summertime's delight.
The constant work of bumble bee
Is such a joy to hear and see
And what a pleasure when we spy
A brightly coloured butterfly
But most of all that special thrill
When blackbird sings his merry trill
As thrushes, robins, linnets too
Join in beneath those skies of blue.

How wonderful how truly fine
That earth is blest with flowers divine
But summer time is often wet
A fact that we must not forget.
For if we had no storms or showers
How could we praise those lovely flowers?
And as the evenings softly fall
We harken to the owl's quaint call.
Then as we watch the bat in flight
We sense the peace of summer's night.

Juliet C Eaton

APRIL FURY

Earth obliterated
By a blanket of snow,
Yesterday there were spring flowers
Jewel colours aglow.
Today, headless and tattered,
Tulips struggle to rise
Towards glowering skies -
And a blackbird sings.

In the rampaging storm
Blossoms fall and soar,
Yesterday's fir rose proud and tall,
Now, heavily, achingly, curving o'er,
Branches frantically lash,
Chimneys groan, trees crash -
Still the blackbird sings.

Where are lambs newly born
And fledglings alike -
Creatures of marshland, moors,
Hedgerows and dyke?
For their fragile security
Dominant gale has no pity.

And no other bird
Through the snow have I heard -
But a brave ruffled blackbird - singing.

Mary Felce

THE BEST ARTIST

There's Titian, and there's Rembrandt,
  creating colours, so divine,
but neither of these artists
  can make pictures quite as fine
as can Old Mother Nature
  with her, oh, so subtle brush -
she takes her time - we breathless wait -
  she doesn't like to rush!
Then - there it is - where're you look,
  where're you turn your head,
colours abound, from palest pink
  right through to magenta red.
The velvet down on roses,
  the *glow* of autumn's sheen,
the glistening of rain on leaf, and
  such glorious shapes are seen.
The sparkling emerald neck of duck,
  kingfisher's royal blue,
the lovely coloured garden birds,
  just to name a few.
The speckled interplay of sun
  on feathered forest trees -
the shaded blend of sunlight
  on striped jerseys of the bees!
And when it comes to rainbows
  her full palette does she use,
she splashes it across the sky
  in all its vibrant hues.

Joyce Hockley

ODE TO THE ALBATROSS

Unfurl your wings and take to flight,
O wanderer of mystery;
soar 'pon wings black and white,
o'er ocean's flowing poetry.
Fly into sunset's fading hues,
through nocturne's starry night;
glide o'er ocean's mystic blues,
when dawn brings forth the light.
To some you are an aimless miracle,
the ocean's faithful sentry;
who navigates the Arctic Circle,
who knows where lies your destiny?
You fly the ocean's wilderness,
feed whilst on the wing;
do you feel the sun's warm caress,
or the Arctic's icy sting?
Some ocean-goers are truly blessed,
when they meet you out at sea;
for you appear without request,
O flying mystery.
Day and night 'neath Heaven's cover,
you soar for weeks on end;
you are the ocean's greatest lover,
to man; a mysterious friend.
So fly on, O flying mystery,
captivate the blue;
you were not created for the sea,
but the sea was made for you.

Ray Varley

RAINBOW (RONDEAU)

Rainbow tinctures arching glow
Iridescent in their bow.
Azure in the heaven's blue,
spectrum in soap-bubble's hue
mirror here on earth below
Rainbow.

Red of sunset's fiery glow,
autumn leaves of orange show,
greenest grass of Lincoln's hue
gentian of deepest blue
turning soon to indigo,
Rainbow.

Modest violets will show,
purple heather swift will flow
over barren spaces new.
All will show their colours true
following in Nature's clue:
Rainbow.

Geraldine Squires

TREES

Sighing softly, gently, flutter flow,
Leaves tremor, as the wind does blow,
On the boughs, are birds in nests,
They're taking a morning rest.

Roaring, squalling, gale force gush,
Rain on the trees, quickly rush,
Back and forth, in a whirl,
Falling leaves, to the ground, hurl.

The sun, so high, from the ground,
Submit, warm rays, all around,
Vapours, from trees, drying out,
Arise, slowly, wafting about.

Once again, the tree leaves, spreading,
When winter comes, they'll be shedding,
The snow, soon, will come, hither and dither,
The shivering leaves, die and wither.

Underground, so snug and deep,
Next year seedlings, are fast asleep,
On boughs of trees, are buds, so tight,
Will appear, again, with spring sunlight.

Gladys Brunt

CHASING THE WIND

We came by air, before
crossing the land, and
finally took to the sea
to chase the wind, to
follow in the footsteps of
Morgan, Drake and Raleigh.

Above the wide expanse
of blue, to a land of
verdant green, with
mulatto, black, white and
more that is the breath of
this ancient scene.

Michael Kennedy

THE SENSES

To define the colours of the rainbow's arc,
Watch stars twinkling in the dark,
See the wonder of birds in flight,
Make me thankful for my sense of sight.

To listen to birds twitter all day long,
Recognise the skylark by its song,
Join the crowd chanting and cheering,
Make me thankful for my sense of hearing.

To breathe in the odour of new mown hay,
Catch the fragrance as flowers sway,
Inhale the aroma of hops as they swell,
Make me thankful for my sense of smell.

To roll wines slowly around my tongue,
Chew on meat when it has been hung,
Devour my favourite food in haste,
Make me thankful for my sense of taste.

To walk through heaps of fallen leaves,
Handle the webs a spider weaves,
Stroke cats that I love so much,
Make me thankful for my sense of touch.

To think an event has happened before,
Sense I am ruled by an out-of-space law,
Predict the outcome when I'm in a fix,
Make me thankful for my 'sense number six'.

Jean Grainger

FIRE OVER VERGELEGEN

A strange, mysterious light shines
Behind the vast mountain range;
The soaring peaks and jagged heights
Are silhouetted against the fiery sky.
Too far away to hear
Is the roar of the conflagration
As it rampages through the bush.
The sky reflects the fearsome furnace
With a deceptive air of tranquillity
And silvered smoke floats upward
Caught in a beam of sunlight.

To the west the hills lie hidden,
Obscured by a pall of caustic cloud.
But from their vanished peaks
The ridges, running downward,
Resemble the trunks of the elephants
Which once roamed freely in this land.

Darkness descends upon the unfolding drama.
Throughout the night the wind howls
And the harsh whisper of rustling leaves
Comes borne on a sea of scorching air.
Ears strain in the darkness
To catch the sound of approaching flames.
Weariness, at length, overcomes the listener
Who succumbs to an uneasy sleep.
Only the Alsation outside the bedroom door
Lies listening, alert to present danger.
The shutters at the window mute the sobbing gale.

Tomorrow, when it comes, will show the sequel;
Expose the damage done to saddened eyes
And hopefully confirm that Vergelegen,
Now danger's passed, survives
To oversee the restoration
And watch as tree and bush once more arise.

Margaret Kunzlik

WINTER

Hark hear the wind
Binding the earth
In chains of iron
Chilling the breath
Trees it bends
Rivers it freezes
Not a bit like summer breezes
Full of ice rain and snow
Where it comes from no-one knows
The wind howls sternly
With relentless power
Hammering and pushing against my door
While by my fire I sit and listen
So cosy and warm I count my blessings.

Maureen E Smith

SUMMERTIME

Summertime gladness begins anew,
Skylarks are scaling the cloudless blue,
Meadowlands shine with a golden glaze
That marks the arrival of buttercup days!

Beeches are flaunting their summer gowns,
Green is the grass on the rolling downs,
Tender the voice of the purling stream
Where the kingfisher darts
and the willows dream.

Wondrously warm is the wind that blows,
Sweet is the scent of the wayside rose,
Carefree the spirit and buoyant the stride
Through the magical moments
of summer tide.

Ursula M Prout

INVISIBLE GARDENER

Who is it plants the woodland flowers,
the daisy, foxglove and bluebell,
Who nurtures them hour upon hour
on mountain, hill and fell.

Who was it planted the mighty trees
and tends them for centuries long,
Who made the denizens of the seas
Leviathans huge and strong.

Who make the birds of the air
and dressed them in raiment splendid
Who placed the mountains here and there,
and his work is never ended.

Who puts the chicks in the nest,
and cubs into the earthen den,
Who made the sun go east and west,
and tomorrow do it all again.

Who fills the sky with fluffy clouds,
and dots the hills with sheep
Who causes thunder, fierce and loud,
and the rumbles in the deep.

Who is this invisible gardener, then?
there's no need to jibber and jabber,
His name is known to mice and men,
Lord God, The Creator, Abba.

William Hayles

AUTUMN IMPRESSIONS

Days pass slowly:
stretching winds
tear spent leaves from weakened body . . .
pull onto
drive through
sweep beyond shrivelled grass.

Flowers linger
cling to passing season,
stifling mists obscure
infant frosts sting -

act in unison
with Nature's knowing hand
to shade memory from time past.

Arthur Pickles

ELEMENTAL

The deep, dark velvet of heavy cloud
throbs with the sound of silence, - no bird sings.
Nerves tingle, taut, waiting.
Nature holds its breath, and a primeval sense
gathers in the nostrils, smelling rain
even as the eerie skies grow dense.

Then, almost unexpected, drops one tear,
a large raindrop, single, - hissing as it falls,
then another, and one more:
the heavens open, releasing sound,
the clouds, shuddering, part
and a shining sheet of water hits the ground.

Tiny streams of water funnel once parched earth,
trees bow, their leaves trembling with delight.
Gently the torrent eases, fury spent,
and now birds chirrup, feathers fluffed, with joy imbued.
Above the clouds lighten, gold rimmed now
and earth once more is sweetly fresh, renewed.

Brenda Heath

WOODLAND VESPERS

Evening haunts the wood,
as softened trills of sleepy birds
echo from the branches.

Steel-grey wood pigeons wheel in
on blue of dusk, to coo
a lullaby from ash or oak.

Woodland creatures scurry below;
their shuffling feet treading a
carpet of spongy moss.

Moths on grey laced wings
glide silently
upon the evening air.

The dog fox, roused from slumber
stirs in the undergrowth -
stretches, and prepares to hunt.

Mysterious sounds of twilight
diminish under the glowing stars
and silvered light of rising moon.

Betty Robertson

WINTER (THE CHILLING OF)

In the still of the night, winter arrives
Breathes over the trees, leaving them bare
Covers the fields with a carpet of white
A solitary fox returns to his lair

The wind bites deep and noses glow
A different world is now taking shape
Crystal clear skies and a host of stars
Ice is forming on pond and lake

Hats and gloves are on display
Snow floats down with barely a sound
The river is frozen and people skate
Ghostly footsteps are left on the ground

Icicles form on the edges of rocks
Hats go swirling down the hill
The laughter of children playing on sleighs
Warm, despite the winter chill

Now the thaw has really begun
Slowly the wind loses its sting
Ice has melted, rivers flow
It won't be long before it's spring

Barry L J Winters

IN THE HEAT OF THE DAY

The stillness is unreal!
So soft is the air;
Not a branch or flower swaying -
Not a whisper anywhere . . .

The bees and blueflies darting -
Echoed on silence is their hum;
From flower to flower hovering,
And back again they come . . .

These rare and precious moments
Extend to one and all,
Like the numbness of the lonely;
Like the falling of a star . . .

Then a raindrop falls from heaven
From a silent passing cloud;
And the rumble in the distance
Can be heard, but not too loud . . .

Now the flowers begin a moving;
Branches begin to sway;
And the birds are homeward coming
With the changing of the day . . .

Suddenly all is run asunder
As the thunder comes on loud;
And the lightning-flashes glowing
Through the ever-darkening cloud . . .

The wildlife of the valley
All huddle from the storm;
Or seek a hasty shelter -
As the shepherd to the barn . . .

Then when the vehemence is all over -
The wet earth cooled and fresh -
All the creatures of this haven
Will rejoice in one loud breath . . .

Mary Pauline Winter

THE ARTISTRY OF THE WIND

The wind whistles through the sand dunes
creating a roaring medley of tunes
forming ripple-waves of arcing lines
artistically drawn across massive inclines.
Footsteps of man made only minutes before
vanish as the mighty wind obliterates the eye-sore
other debris cast by ignoramuses aside
taken by the gusts and carried far and wide
each grain an element of creation
countless and blinding in a palette of sophistication.
How insignificant is man among these mighty hills
here the force of nature counteracts all human wills.

John M O'Sullivan

A GENTLE BREEZE

A gentle breeze coming from the sea
Is nice and cool you see
But any kind of weather could follow it
Like rain falling down on me.

A gentle breeze coming from the sea
Is it the calm before the storm?
For it is suddenly getting colder
Certainly not warm.

A gentle breeze coming in from the sea
Is nice at the end of a hard day
Maybe it will last all night
So I can get some sleep hurray.

Keith L Powell

WINTER'S BLAST

The weary winter is coming fast,
And soon will come the winter's blast,
The groaning trees will shed their leaves,
And stand naked and bare in the icy breeze,
Winter's chill will blow angry and cold,
In the sky now clouds will unfold,
Then descends the chilly smothering snow,
Driven by the gusting winds as they blow,
Old Jack Frost will turn the earth cold and white,
While in the night sky, the moon and stars shine bright,
Ice will cover the ponds, streams and rivers,
While the earth grows icy cold and shivers,
The icy wind will blow and groan,
And chill your body right through to the bone.

A J Young

SPIRIT OF AFRICA

Majestic form
a silhouette
the backdrop
setting sun,
as dusk envelops
night time stirs
to take control
'til morning comes.
A world of darkness
reigns supreme
as night time creatures roam,
illuminated eyes of green
are all in shadows
that are seen.
Beneath black velvet
night time sky
the hunters stalk their prey,
as deadly
as the predators
that hunt by light of day.
Majestic form
the silhouette
stirs gently
where he lies.
As dawn approaches
night retreats
submits
to opalescent skies.

Michael Cheney

THE GARDEN

Thank You God for the soft green leaves
That dance on tall majestic trees
Thank You God for the flowers that grow
From the tiny seeds we plant below
Thank You God for the grass so green
And the daisies that pop up in between.
Thanks for the pond where the fishes hide
And cats and birds drink side by side.
We hear the children playing nearby
Enjoying the sun and the clear blue sky
On balmy evenings there's smoke in the air
The BBQ's on, so we know Dad's there.
Sausages sizzle and burgers burn.
The onions are crisp, it's done to a turn.
The garden gives pleasure to many a man
Who tends and cares as much as he can.
Even in winter when all looks bleak
While over all a vigil You keep
When things look dark and all colour is gone
We'll give thanks and wait for the cuckoo's song.

Joyce M Carter

WINTER'S REST

Dapple shades of an autumn day
Adorn the trees along the way
Golden leaves without a sound
Floating softly to the ground.

A blanket soon beneath your arch
Will lay until the winds of March
Like confetti falls to waters grey
Will drift until they float away

No longer are you host of trees
For birds, butterflies, or honey bees
You rest while winter plays its games
For awake you come in springtime rains

Once more you'll wear a gown of green
Many shades of silk with pretty sheen
So proud and stately you will stand
Until God's creatures gather round

Susan Goldsmith

SUNRISE

The sky is bright with hues of red and gold
Its brilliance almost dazzling to behold
The leaves are gently fluttering in the breeze
And birds are sweetly singing in the trees
As at this wonderland I stop and gaze
My heart is filled with thankfulness and praise
For all creation, and the One who made
The sky, the sea, the peaceful woodland glade
The hills the mountains, fields, the lambs at play
The birds that sing so sweetly day by day
The rivers as they flow through countrysides
And oh so many other gifts besides.

Doris Prowse

GOLDEN DAYS

The wind whispered through the trees
And brushed their leaves with open hands
The sun warmed the earth
In rays of golden bands.
Shadows falling on shimmering blades of grass
Wings of birds dart through the shadows as they pass
Through rays of golden sun
See blue skies and clouds all having fun
Moving swiftly passing by
Like white sails high up in the sky

Christine Hervin

THE RAINBOW

Raindrops glistening through the sun,
Picking up colours one by one.
Blues, pinks, green and yellow,
Pretty colours that will mellow.
Violet, indigo and orange glow
Across the sky is the rainbow

J Vail

AUTUMN

Winter now well on its way.
Migrant birds, they do not stay.

The old oak tree sheds a bough.
Quickly changing seasons now.

Starlings flock, and swoop on high
At dusk, collect, to fill the sky.

Jay's distinctive jerky flight,
A clown of a bird, with colours bright.

As winter spreads her cold damp mantle,
Trees and hedges, now leaves dismantle.

Rook and jackdaw fly from perch
It's now for acorns, they must search.

Flying insects, almost gone.
Most of the birds have lost their song.

It's now we haven't long to go
Before dear Nature spreads her snow.

Tiny Longfellow

BORN TO BE FREE

Powerful white stallion, you reign supreme,
Your freedom your heaven, the moors your dream
No reins or saddle to burden your back
Just the wind's soft breath along a woodland track
Born to be proud and be free all your days
To run with the wind, or in sun just to laze
To swim in the stream, to cool the heat of your soul
To be the proud father of your unborn foal
The king of your race, you should always be free
No chains as your master, no man with a key
So run with the breeze, lift your head proud
Be wild, untamed, the master of your ground

Sue Starling

TAKE CARE

Please don't disturb the compost heap,
There might be a hedgehog fast asleep!
He's all curled up in a prickly ball
And nobody knows he's there at all.
So, till he wakes, and out does creep
Please don't disturb the compost heap.

In spring we all rush out to play
In gardens, on a sunny day.
But won't you listen to my pleas
To never, ever, climb in trees?
For tiny chicks up in their nest
Are trying hard to get some rest.

Don't chase the pretty butterfly
Because his beauty caught your eye.
He'll die before the day is out
And then the world will be without
Another creature, dead and gone.
If you persist there'll soon be none.

If we all take care together
We can teach our friends to see,
That the lovely world we live in
Is not just for you and me,
And then you will be proud to say
'I've helped my world survive today.'

V Francis

PATIENT THOUGHTS

I sat here watching patiently
In case that I should see
A movement in the grasses
Or a bird high in a tree

I looked in vain for butterflies
At last! What did I spy?
That quite elusive creature
The lovely dragonfly.

The thing that was unusual
No water was in sight
It was a thing I'd talked about
A lot, the other night.

Next came a thing of beauty
I'd seen one once before
A large bright coloured butterfly
Just flew right in the door

I put it outside gently
To harm it was not on
I don't know where it went to
One moment here, then gone.

Mary M Aris

LEAVES

All sorts of patterns to see,
Shades of green varying with one another.
What about the ivy? With a serrated edge,
The different shades of green mingling together.
Dragonflies are hovering over the lily pads.
Out comes a frog and sits on a great leaf,
When a shower comes
Some leaves hold the dews for the insects.
Then the upright sword of the lily
And also the daffodil leaf so narrow.
Sunlight dapples through the leaves,
Of all the different trees
Sun warms the ground for the plants.
So out come all the little leaves
Followed by the flowers.
All the different colours
Mingling together over God's earth.
The velvety leaf of an African violet
Prickly holly leaves, with red berries
And shimmering green leaves.
The spiky needles of a fir tree,
Drooping leaves of a willow,
Hairy leaves of a carnivorous plant
Golden leaves in autumn.
Different shades in all their glory.
Falling to the earth to enrich the soil.
But *hey presto!* The next spring
Little buds appear everywhere!
Yes! The leaves have a glory all of their own . . .

Margaret Pearce

As They Play

The seeds I sow
in very straight rows,
into flowers soon grow
with the help of rain and sunshine.
The grass is green
and it's a beautiful scene
as I look and lean
our of my bay window.
Now there's fine weather
the children shout with pleasure.
Their happiness rings out in laughter
as on the swings they play.
Their friends come to join our picnic
with cakes and biscuits and ice-creams to lick
and bread and butter, cut quite thick.
There's more than enough to go round.
The TV's on
the cartoons fun
one more to watch,
then off to bed at nine o'clock.
The sleepy-heads
tucked up in bed, their stories read,
say night night, sweet dreams and God bless.

Rosemary Medland

NATURE'S WISDOM

All quiet and still is this time of night when
thoughts of our mind go into the deep - what
changes take place with the passing of time -
darkness of night when I went into sleep - and
the wonder of light again as I awake to see
a new day of life - Nature's ways have to be
obeyed and in her wisdom she has made
rules she calls night and day.

Roland-Patrick Scannell

RAINBOW RHYMES

Early spring opens with brush strokes of yellow
Cowslip and daffodil dance in the meadow
Ponds reflect kingcups, celandines shimmer,
Dewy-faced buttercups glisten and shiver.
Violet and speedwell add touches of blue
And carpets of bluebells drench woodlands anew.
Sunshine through rain paints a glorious rainbow
To arch the grey sky and gild the green hedgerow.

In summer our gardens splash crimson and gold
With roses, and orange of bold marigold.
But when autumn hurries her scurrying leaves
And martins are gone from their nests in the eaves,
Elder's rich wine - a deep glowing purple -
Kindles the plumage of starlings. They sparkle!
When white winter's hiding her pearls - mistletoe
She wipes the slate clean with a fresh fall of snow.

So when springtime's ready with sunshine and rain,
Pass light through a prism. Start painting again!

Veronica Ross

THE WEB OF LIFE

A cobweb glistened in the morning dew
A silver silhouette against sky blue
The builder of this marvel could not be seen
Just the shimmering thread of where she'd been

One broken thread on which the dew shone
Was it the scene where a victim long gone
Had fought and lost the battle for life
Predator and captive tangled in strife?

I considered my weaving as through life I tread
Could I account for every broken thread?
Unlike my Lord, I a predator could become
But He, as a sheep before her shearers was dumb

A new web is woven, a new day is born
I pray that today no threads will be torn
Our God as the builder, is Himself unseen
But evidence abounds where the Creator has been

John Remmington

RIVERS

Rivers rushing from the hills,
To the fertile lands below,
Splashing over rocks and stones,
Ever gurgling, fast or slow.

Fed by tiny trickling streams,
Make fine music, and it seems
That murmuring wind adds to the sound
Of drizzling rain upon the ground.

Ever on they seem to flow,
Even on through mist and snow.
Quickly through the land they go
To the valleys far below.

Diane Mackintosh

NATURE'S LOVE

Constant ever-changing moods,
Autumn, winter, summer, spring,
See nature's true creation,
Birds always on the wing.
Trees so very special,
Always changing hue,
With each and every season,
Shades will always give a clue.
A bluebell wood in springtime,
Glorious to behold,
The wonder of a poppy field,
So striking yet so bold.
Oh, the majesty of mountains,
Rivers flowing to the sea,
Vast expanse of moorland,
Subtle beauty wild and free.
Without nature's love around us,
Oh yes we know for sure,
The quality of all our lives,
Would indeed be very poor.

Dorothy M Gillway

REFLECTIONS

The mist rose gently o'er the lake to cloud the water's edge
Where geese had neatly built their nests 'midst rushes and the sedge
And common wagtails searched for flies beneath each jaggèd ledge.

Tall Scottish pines across the hill exuded heavy scent
Their needles deepening the soil hid cartridges well-spent
And fallow deer around the woods crushed ferns where'ere they went.

Buttercups and daisies grew with other meadow flowers
Near fairly pleasant walking by fields of Friesian cows
And dreams became reality 'neath nature's willow boughs.

Another path by shading trees led to a deeper lake
Where diving birds would fish and swim alongside duck and drake
And thoughts of these affect my soul as if my heart would break.

For though the countryside near here is flecked with oak and lime
These cannot ever take the place of firs and fragrant thyme
And feeling thus will ne'er erase fond memories of mine.

K M Blackwood

BREEZE

The breeze unsettled the
timing of life
but lifted through the trees
the yearning for newness.
As it moved, the shimmering leaves
beckoned to the sunshine in autumn
and so the yearning for newness did cease.
The snows of the winter did sparkle
as the 'breeze' again unsettled the air
but lifting to the sunlight through a rainbow
the breeze let the snow become rain.
Unanswered as the clouds were that moment
to the breezes of life spun in times of high life;
the breeze gently sifted and folded
and brought a great calm to the seas.

Jackie Callinan

AUTUMN LEAVES

Leaves are falling to the ground,
  swirling softly, hardly a sound.
In the morning breeze they flutter,
  laying forlornly, in the gutter.
In the parks and in the town,
  laying where they have tumbled down.
In a puddle, one does ponder,
  until a breeze takes it yonder.
The colours and hues as they fall,
  off the trees that stand so tall.
Oranges, red, brown and green,
  the autumn colours can be seen.
Through the countryside is the best,
  crunching leaves as we head west.
Walking through the fallen leaves,
  like a carpet beneath the trees.

Sandra Houghton

REFLECTIONS

Through the days you've grown to be
My constant source of company
My every thought, my every prayer
My every waking moment share
Your smiles, your dreams and sometimes pain
The tears that fall like summer rain
As the evening shadows softly unfold
These dreams and hopes for thee I hold
In the quiet lull of early dawn
A brand new day of strength is born
As the weeks turn into golden years
We'll remember the sorrow and the tears
In the circle of life, an echo in time
Like the circle of seasons all entwined
Spring's fleeting touch this earth to bless
The warmth of summer's sweet caress
Mellow autumn's harvest glow
To winter's frost and pure white snow

Sylvia Partridge

WISHING

If on this earth another life I spend,
And choice am given,
I'd like to be a bird.

To graceful flight my skills I'd bend,
By breezes driven,
And cries of comrades heard.

Stephen R Ramsden

THE WIND

Fly overhead and through the trees.
Bend the reeds, and uproot poppies.
Toss great boulders, high, through the air,
And strip the trees completely bare.
Whistle and moan and send a chill.
Someone will shiver at your will.

And carry with you as you go
Thousands of seeds that you will sow.
Grizzle and moan and toss and turn
To catch the softness of the fern.
Then you can show your gentler side
As everyone has to abide.

And as someone closes the door
Whisk it open with a huge roar.
And there, in the hallway, you see
The dancing leaves, thrown from the trees,
Tossing and turning as if alive,
At the mercy of your loud cries.

'Who's there?' someone timidly calls
As the door flaps to the wall.
No-one appears. No-one is there.
It's only a cold rush of air
To caress your face, comb your hair,
And go from whence it came - nowhere.

Doreen King

THE WEATHER WATCHER

We may travel around this world;
To see many wonders slow unfurled;
Forests, woods, trees in number,
In winter all except evergreen in slumber.
Cool winds of spring may touch our face,
In summer heat holds us in its embrace,
Autumn's challenge is colour quite grand,
Winter again gripping like iron band.
The seasons pass and repeat again;
Sun on sun, wind on wind, rain on rain.
Mountain, hill, furrow and field,
All in turn changing shades revealed.
Offer up your thanks and appreciation,
That you live in such a climatic nation.
Wish every day that the weather may alter . . .
But hope the natural balance of all things
             . . *May never falter.*

Michael Childs

THE WATERFALL

God gave us eyes that we might see
the wonderful world he made.
All creatures of our God and King
the beautiful water cascade.

Torrents rushing down the rock face
rapidly reaching the base.
Then calming, meets the surging waves
now a gentle rivulet chase.

Reflections in the stream that flows
a prism of colours rare.
Together running just as one
such harmony and peace to share.

The trickling brook meanders far
many fine stories to tell.
The rainbow shades we often see
remind us that all will be well.

We thank you Lord with all our hearts
for this cataract we see.
Your caring hands, love, hope and warmth
ever flowing from you so free.

Margaret Jackson

THE BEACH

The beach is deserted this early in the morning,
even the gulls have stayed at home.
Only the sea is awake . . .
and I.

So I cast off my clothes in a frenzy,
and chase the breeze to the sea.
The turn-tide frills around my ankles,
beckoning, beckoning me.

The desire to strike out for the breakers,
just to prove I can master the sea,
drags me in, jumpy and skittish
and free, and free.

But soon I feel fingers teasing, teasing,
shifting the grains at my feet.
Yet, still I search the blue-mist
for dreams, just out of reach.

Then, wide-eyed I sense the menace looming,
see its shroud closing in.
Too late! I am taken . . . pounded, beaten
then flung like flotsam
upon the silent, silent beach.

Sue Hansard

MAKING THE MOST OF IT

It's a funny old world we live in
    Nothing like the past
Some corrupted people
    With drugs and sin
Youngsters at night
    Filled with whiskey and gin.

Yet I feel as tho'
    I've landed on top of an Xmas tree
With all its glitter and glo'
    And me being with all the angels
Doing a lovely talent show.

I was near to the end
    But now on the mend
My eyes sparkle my heart filled with pride
    Dear God no more will I ever hide

A poem of mine hangs on the wall
    As I gaze towards it I feel so tall
The hospital staff have done wonders for me
    Thoughts in my scripts
I collect by walking along by the sea

Yes everyone's so friendly
    I couldn't ask for more
I wait for the postman
    As I get letters galore
Yes I'm making the most of it.

Lilian Thorne

WHERE DOES THE WIND COME FROM

Where does the wind come from? Where does the wind go?
On deserts so arid and lands veiled in snow;
Atop the high mountains; in valleys below;
Where does the wind come from? Where does the wind go?

It blows through the trees with a rustling sound.
It ripples the grass growing low on the ground.
It tosses the seas in the ocean so vast
And throws up the waves; then on the beach cast.

It eddies round corners with gust and with blast.
It chases the clouds through the sky oh, so fast.
It dances the leaves as they twirl and they whirl
Till they land on the ground where the wind dost them hurl.

In storms that are violent, it uproots massive trees
And sink lonely boats in the heaving grey seas.
From the home laundry line it blows clothes newly washed
And on wet muddy ground clean linen is tossed.

The wind brings us sunshine. The wind brings us rain.
It helps, through creation, our lives to sustain.
It blows seeds to the ground that then they may grow
That we may have sust'nance on this good earth below.

If we didn't have wind then we wouldn't have rain;
Just mist on the ground our plants to maintain.
For the heat of the sunshine and the warmth of God's love
As He guides us so surely to His heaven above.

M M Sherwood

WATERS UNCONFINED AS MIRRORS

The sea stretches off into the far distance.
Today it is calm and peaceful and the
Sun shines on it, reflecting all its glory on
The smooth surface. You can see it
Reflected on the surface as smooth as
Glass while at night the moon does
The same but not with the same intensity.
Beside the lake grow the trees which cast their
Shadows on the still waters and the hills, too,
Peep over their tops to be reflected on
The calm surface. But when the storm blows,
Only the grey clouds are reflected on their
Surfaces as Nature scowls in anger as
The rain unsettles the once calm areas.
But like all else, the storm settles down,
Blows itself out and once more
Both shining orbs are seen on the crystal clear
Surface, not the angry tossing and heaving but
The calm stillness of a summer's day as
Quiet, clear, still and peaceful as
The surface of mirrors.

Thomas W Splitt

THE STORM

Everything was peaceful, on this bright and sunny day,
Then suddenly a rumble, in the distance far away.
Dark clouds started gathering, a storm was on the way,
Maybe it would pass us by, we could only hope and pray.
The air felt so oppressive, as the sky turned really black,
This would be a bad one, but there was no turning back.
You could see it drawing nearer, as it came right overhead,
Please let is pass us quickly, for these types of storms we dread.
Then came a flash of lightning, that lit up all the sky,
My wife she started trembling, and I knew the reason why.
Then came an almighty bang, as we looked out to see,
A thunderbolt had struck and split, the lovely old oak tree.
Hail and rain came lashing down, it seemed to last for hours,
Followed by more lightning, then intermittent showers.
Very soon it went away, the air felt fresh and clear,
And with it went the feeling, of everything we fear.
So when a storm breaks overhead, what can you expect,
Do as we have always done, and treat it with respect.

W Kitson

THE COTTAGE GARDEN

I was walking along a leafy country lane one fine day,
It was summer and the fields were full of ripening hay.
And then I saw it a most wonderful sight,
It made me so happy and my heart felt light.
A little thatched cottage tucked away on its own,
With garden so tidy and a lawn neatly mown.
I stood and I looked my eyes in amaze.
Such riotous colours, it was just ablaze.
With hollyhocks tall, and delphiniums blue,
And round the front door there were red roses too.
Cornflowers, sweetpeas, pansies and sunflowers,
You could sit among them for many happy hours.
Along the little winding path there I saw,
A cat sitting quietly and washing his paw.
In a bed he sat, where forget-me-nots grew,
A lovely sight and what a wonderful hue.
There was a wildflower garden there as well I could see,
For the birds, butterflies, and the humble bumblebee.
Foxgloves, lilies-of-the-valley and the canterbury bell,
They were all there down in that wooded dell.
A stream meandered through this lovely place,
Where swallows flew around there giving chase.
To catch insects to eat while on the wing,
It made me so happy, I could almost sing.
So when I feel lonely, unhappy and sad,
I think of that garden and then I feel glad.
For there before me I saw beauty unfurled,
What lovely things we have in our wonderful world.

Carol Diane Milne

REST AND MOTION

See the hare go leaping
Over the corrugated field.
See the hare go leaping
Like a pip of life squeezed out
By thumb and finger.
See the hare go leaping!
See the hare go leaping
To the right,
To the left
And stopping in its tracks.

(See the hare.)

Meanwhile, above this single point of life,
A hawk hangs suspended in the upper air.

Stan Downing

BROKEN FLOWER

See meadow's sweetest flower,
Trod down by vandal shoe,
Awakes within the hour,
To greet the sun anew.

Attended by nurse nature,
Washed clean by morning dew,
She gains each day in stature,
Dons yet a prettier hue.

With stain and pain now far away,
Her petals full unfurled,
She reigns today in full array,
The loveliest in the world.

The breezes breathe a soft refrain,
To see her blithe and free,
And in a while she smiles again,
A joy for all to see.

Lee Graham

WINTER

February, the coldest month.
Day after day filled with roaring wind.
Ragged, black-edged clouds rush by
in louring, fast-grey skies,
like wild horse in stampede,
fleeing from an unseen threat.

Rooks whip past me overhead,
fighting against the demented, howling sky.
Wings straining to hold the air,
feathers sticking out at painful angles.
Buffeted by the bitter wind,
their cries are torn from open beaks.

Endless bleak and dismal days.
Icy knives sneaking under doors.
Feet and hands brittle with the cold.
The fire hisses softly,
fighting a losing battle,
as it tries in vain to warm my frozen bones.

This is winter, the harsh reality.
Not romantic, snow-filled fields and lanes,
just drab-dull, rain-washed days,
muddy puddles, and streets filled with litter.
Telephone wires whistle dirges for the dead,
and I, sit here alone, aching for the sun.

Gordon Jackson

SONG OF THE WHOOPER SWAN

We travel the world in our search for warm loneliness,
seeking the haven of ice-free meres
where we can live undisturbed,

shunning the species that shelters indoors -
he who's destroying our traditional routes
with ominous structures involving our fate;
we eschew that devilish vandal, the biped.

This patch of water where we feed
becomes a desert in the short nights
when we're back home,
where we see again the grandeur
of the tundra's noble space,
barren, vast, going on forever,
neglected by the human race.

Here Man's summer playground offers
brief escape from gnawing fear.
But August footprints leave their message,
which we still scent in winter air.

Perhaps one day there'll be no spaces
left for even swans to breed in.
Maybe in the distant future
food supplies will all be burned.
Perhaps our wander-freedom's threatened,
eradicating Cygnus ways.

Come apocalypse, millennium,
holocaust or world on fire,
Man's triumphant road through 'Progress'
ends by nullifying desire -
and thus the biped will expire.

Arnold Bloomer

A DAY IN EARLY FEBRUARY

There's a nip in the air
But I don't care!
As I go on my way
For 'a feeling of spring'
- And the joy it will bring,
Makes me 'just walk on air', today!

Catkins are swinging,
And songbirds are singing:
But still traces of snow - where it drifted.
There is warmth in the sun,
For the winter's near done:
And the cloud, hanging over me, 'lifted'!

Gaenor Spratley

SEASONAL HIGHLAND

Snow lies thick on the highland ground
Blood red sunsets most nights are found
Capercaillie perched high in the Scots Pine
This fairy tale landscape I wish it were mine

A fresh highland wind brings buzzards on wing
At ground owls hunt and song thrushes sing
The water is now losing its wintry chill
And soft green shoots emerge to thrill

Summer's here and the air is getting hot
Blooming marsh orchids display all they've got
Pikes out hunting and deer families roam
In this beautiful place, these creatures call home

The heather takes on its autumnal bloom
Stags roar in the misty mountain gloom
Pink footed geese inbound from the iced splinter
Small mammals gather rowans to prepare for the winter.

S R Eaton

THE FIR TREE

So majestic, tall and slim,
Reaching up towards the sky,
Always neat, and tidy, trim,
Quick to grow and slow to die.

Trunk so smooth, and hard, and grey,
Can be used to furnish homes,
To the tree our homage pay,
So distinctive with its cones.

Needles thick, and sharp, and green,
In the wind they blow about,
Such a wondrous sight to see,
'To you God' our thanks we shout.

In many lands fir trees grow,
Seen in countries far and near,
They are seen where e'er you go,
And to us they are so dear.

Suzanne Joy Golding

FROM MY CONSERVATORY

The oak has donned its mantle green,
Fairer than I have ever seen.
While hawthorn near is clothed in white
A cloud of blossom, wondrous light.
The ash still standing strong and tall
Has hardly any leaves at all.
I still can see on branches bare
The birds and squirrels playing there.
Their nests are clear for all to see
And spring seems very close to me.

The garden's green, yet here and there
A splash of colour strikes the air.
Forget-me-nots, their misty blue
Surround the bluebells' colour true.
The wallflowers bring a flash of gold
Their colours always strong and bold.
In pots and baskets spread around
Are primulas and pansies found.
And all this beauty I can see
In peace from my conservatory.

Marjorie Worth

Ocean Views

The moonlight shimmers across this dreamlike sea,
Starlight blinking confirming what peace can be,
Gazing across the ocean's wide expanse,
Observing the swell. The waves in their dance,
Devouring serenity, as long as it can last,
No tidal quick-step, this comes so fast,
Rising and falling this gentle sway,
Reminding us now, it's the end of the day.

Will sleep come, how will sea greet new dawn,
Placid and tame as a timid fawn.

Or, will we experience sea in its glory,
Waves tossing and churning at some inner fury.

Loud the wind screams, joining the tempest,
Fathoms below houses deathlike seductress,
Eruptions at sea bed cause unruly waves,
Unleashing control, no longer conclave,
No respecter of objects impeding its path,
Destruction the aim, at it, sea will laugh,
These changes so witnessed by sea farers all,
Still none can resist the oceanic call.

Elizabeth Eade

TRANQUILLITY

While I sit in my meadow so bright,
  Ever watchful of each tiny mite,
Birds of all species hover close by.
  Oh what a joy to be here
Where peace surrounds us.
  Tranquillity is so rarely found -
Only nature can nourish one's mind -
  When material things seem to distract us
Scurry away to your corner;
  And just dream.

Norma Pusey

THE RESTLESS SEA

The glistening sea stretches out far beyond my vision
Touching my soul by its immensity
In harmony with the gulls
As they make their presence known.
The marble sky peers down from the heavens
As I stand gazing at the horizon in disbelief
Its beauty takes my breath away.
The atmosphere changes with passing time
And clouds of grey darken the skies.
A violent storm shows its anger
And I tremble at the sound of roaring thunder
The sea responds, losing its calm,
And powerful waves begin to toss frantically,
With the sound of panic stricken gulls deafening my ears
I feel no peace or tranquillity
Confused and alone, I sense fear.
But soon the restless sea controls its rage
And after the storm . . . the calm.

Phyllis R Harvey

WHAT COMES NATURALLY

A child is born
Every day
But someone dies as well
Things happen naturally
Who knows who can tell
Animals are born just the same
Nature takes its course
We find ourselves doing things
In a natural kind of way of course
But thanks to our weather
It's natural in every way
Let babes be born
Animals as well
Natural things happen
It's life so they say
Don't be any different
Just be natural
In your own way

Poet P Wardle

SILENCE, AND QUIETLY BE PEACEFUL

The 'Silence' is in the dead of the night,
When all is dark, when there is no light
No birds do sing, or see the trees that sway,
They are seen by all, in the light of day.
When the winds blow, they play their tunes
They break the silence whilst bright is the moon, -
And
Quietly runs the little stream,
As I sit by its side, and 'quietly be'
I'm far from all, for I sit alone, -
Watching the water as it washes o'er the stones;
Wild flowers they're growing entwined among the grass
They would nod their head, - should I pass -
But here I sit, for there's lots to see
All alone, and 'quietly be'. -
And
Then on I walk, still all alone along the shore,
Far from the noise, and people, to me would be a bore,
Comfortable am I in my old clothes,
For I have no need to look my best,
To laze around, or to sit and rest,
I watch the birds, and I hear their cries
'Tis the only sound twixt the sea, and sky,
O'so 'peaceful', though the sky is dull

Leslie F Dukes

FLOURISHING OF A TREE

What a more lovely sight, can there be.
Than the flourishing of a tree,
Tall and lofty arms outstretch
For the birds, to build their nests.

They brighten up the day if it is dull
And keep you dry on a wet day.
Then comes the sun, shining so warm,
The shade is wonderful to all.

Winifred

LAKELAND

Glaciated mounds of greys and browns
Soft scenes of velvet greens
Dovetailed together by bracken and heather
Stone-stitched with meandering seams.

Dark silent waters sit patient and wait
for winter's arterial flow.
Brisk clouds with their shadows en route to elsewhere
massage all contours below.

Ant like figures with various vigours
booted and back-packed in trails
move with a mission to glean a true vision
from peak upon peak over dales.

Sudden swirls from moist hanging mist
blending all shades of split fell.
This cold camouflage chills human endeavour,
affirms nature's power so well.

Peter Cocker

CHANGING RHYTHMS AND RHYMES . . .

Only the wind is listening
Stars in the heavens too
The moon with its silvery symbol
In time, will reach out to you
Why consult the cosmos
to understand
What we must face
Learning only today, what tomorrow
will teach
To, trust and wait
Only the wind is listening
As, I trace sketches in your name
Hills of your native land
shall hear, from me, echoes of
Those past times again
Now it's only a quickstep
Changing rhythms and rhymes
Eventuality of being . . . if not seeing, a land that
reached out and cried.

Sharon R Halsey

THE COUNTRY PARK

Through the bare trees,
Leaden skies can be seen.
Through the network of branches,
With their foliage mean,
Shedding dim light
On the dampness below,
As searching for sustenance
Squirrels scurry to and fro.
Small children are squealing,
Ducks are after the bread
While the coots hover hopefully
Leftovers to be fed.
Rotting twigs crack,
Sturdy boots are a must,
As the thick cloying earth,
The pathways encrust.
But couples stroll round,
Huddled arm in arm
Remembering the summertime,
And the park's quiet charm.

L Pigrome

SPRING EQUINOX

It can't be spring, just can't be spring,
Even though days are lengthening.
That bitter, cold, Siberian blast
Is saying winter isn't past.
The frozen pond, the frosty grass,
That icy lacing on the glass,
Those leaden skies with threat of snow,
All signs of winter these, I know,
And yet, and yet -
Crocuses spread their mauve and gold,
They don't seem to notice the cold!
Daffodils defiantly dance,
They're not afraid to take their chance.
Primroses brighten up the hedge,
While buds swell on each black twig's edge,
Catkins dangle and blackbirds sing -
I guess it really must be spring!

Eleanor Rogers

WINDY

The sun coming up on the eastern moor
with an early red sky, there'll be a storm for sure,
Mares tails above with a quickening breeze,
the birds taking shelter in the now bending trees.

Down on the beach the sand starts to shift,
while along in the harbour there's a boat adrift,
in another hour there will be quite a blow,
'Oh look! Someone's taken that boat in tow.'

The seagulls stick their heads to the wind,
while the wagtails and jackdaws have shelter to find,
the spray blows off of the choppy crests
and the last boat to harbour has come to rest.

Force nine they said was the forecast today,
so the kids won't be down to swim or play,
we'll just sit and watch the spume fly about,
and by the end of the day the storm will die out.

Just before sunset the storm has now passed,
we knew from the start that it wouldn't last,
but now the sky has turned a glorious red,
it'll be nice in the morning - so let's go to bed.

R Gardner

THE LARK

My heart leaps up to reach your melting notes,
Heaven's rafters ring with your inspir'd song.
Within it I find all of summer's joy
And thrill at all the life encapsul'd there.
Can I infer the motive that drives you
To be the one that makes my wonderment
At all the glories of the earth below
And all the dazzling blue of sky above?
That one small bird can so much rapture show
When it possesses nothing of world's goods
Nor all the treasures men do value so,
Leaves me as humble as you e'er remain.
Whilst I can hearken to your ecstasy
I know that worth is measured not in time
Nor space, but only in the divine spark
Of every creature's everlasting soul.

John Pottinger

LOYALTY

Little dog so loyal, true
What does life hold for you
A new master and new home
New things to do, new fields to roam
Lots of love and lots of licks
That's the way your body ticks

Little dog so loyal, true
Early life's not good for you
A new master and new home
A broken leg, heart rending moan
Lots of beatings, lots of kicks
That's the way your master ticks.

Little dog so loyal, true
Life has turned, it's good to you
People rally to your aid
Cruelty's over, be not afraid
Another new master, another new home.
And my what's this, a 'special' bone.

Eileen Torkington

TOWNIE

A glimpse of country life
Relief from daily strife
Walk in the park
Sun blazing down
A relaxing few hours
Change from life in town
Families passing hours away
Walking through the grounds
Hear all the different noises
Not recognising some of the sounds.
Used to hustle bustle
So busy, never hear branches rustle
Cars and trains all around
Plants, trees and wildlife there's none to be found.

Janette Harazny

FELLED TREES

The trees had been felled;
The leaves no longer
Allowed to fall.

The shelter they made
Had been taken away
From all the birds
Who'd nested,
          nestled,
                    sheltered.

Many generations
Had been conceived
Amongst the shelter
Of their leaves
But now

The trees had been felled
The leaves no longer
Allowed to fall.

Andrina Keeling

THE MANY FACES OF NATURE

Nature it has many faces, sometimes it smiles then it grimaces.
See the sun kissed dew upon a petal, or the lightning as it strikes metal.
Look at the sea as a millpond still, the crashing waves they have power to kill.
Watch as mother duck leads her bairns, always respect the monsoon rains.
See the lioness playing with her cubs, she has sharp claws still covered in blood.
Enjoy a sunset on a vast wide plain, watch the tornado as it brings many pain.
Bask in the sun on a sunny Cyprus beach, then an earthquake puts your children out of reach.
Yes nature it has many faces I have found, it can kill without a single sound.
Just accept nature and her moods, and be thankful that you have food.

Don Goodwin

My Thanks To A Rainbow

When I see a rainbow what do I see?
All the different colours, and what they mean to me.

I take the pink from the rainbow, and wrap myself in it
Just like a cosy blanket, a warm and perfect fit.

And then I take the yellow, the colour of the sun,
So bright and gay and happy, a colour full of fun

The red is the next colour. To me it seems to shout
Use its powerful energy, it's what life's all about

And sometimes I will take the blue, when I am feeling low
I bathe myself in its colour, and soon I'm on the go

The green from the rainbow brings balance to my life
And under its gentle influence I live with joys or strife

And then there is the purple, a mix of reds and blue
So deep and oh so holy, with its majestic hue

So when I see a rainbow, high up in the sky
I see a cylinder of colour to live my life by.

Pauline Carroll

THE SILVERY TAY

A poet wrote of the silvery Tay
they chided, laughed at what he had to say
If you can imagine the morning sunrise
a large orange ball, a splendid surprise

Then at sunset going down on the river
amazing scenes send a shiver
All the contrast over the bridge
road and railway seem to merge

Yachts, speedboats, water skiing
tugboats, tankers, lifeboat, screaming
Oil platforms a magnificent sight
especially when lit up at night

A few of the sights Magonagol would wonder
knowing his poems I'm sure he would ponder
You have to live by the silvery Tay
to appreciate the beauty God gives everyday . . .

Jean Tennent Mitchell

MAY MORNING

When acorns are greening on the oaks
And rabbits bobbing in the briars,
Radiant as a rainbow
Newly awakened from dreams,
Comes the Green Lady on swallow's wings,
Attended by sunshine and showers
In the golden May morning.
Where she treads the earth will bloom
With woodruff, wild rose and celandine,
Anemone, tansy and teasel,
Marigold and meadowsweet,
Feverfew and saxifrage.
When catkins are dancing in the breeze
And brown hares leaping beneath the trees
In summer's enchanted realm,
Crowned with sweet honeysuckle
The Green Lady will begin her reign
Under an apple blossom bower
In the golden May morning
When the earth is green with life.

Denise Margaret Hargrave

THE FIRST FROST

The first frost comes and autumn breathes a sigh of things to come,
The birds fly south to warmer parts and the hedgehog scurries home.
All nature takes on a rosy glow with leaves of red and gold
And badgers deep within their sets prepare for icy cold.
The moon looks twice the size at night and stars glow all around
Then nature takes a well earned rest while winds and rain abound.
So cut the logs and light the fire and make the room alight
With glowing embers in the hearth and dancing candlelight.
For we too will take our turn to shelter in our homes
To share the warmth of family love, safe and not alone.

Stuart R Firth

SUMMER PROMISE

Did you see the dew glistening on the grasses,
And the gossamer silken threads of spiders' webs,
Did you smell the early morning freshness,
No smoking chimneys, no polluted air,
Feel a benign breeze quivering on skin and hair,
Inquisitively rustling among the flowers,
While the long awaited sun streams down pure gold,
Unfolding shadows.

Betty Eileen Houghland

CASTOR HANGLANDS

Uninvited to those still and ancient Hanglands
from Roman days or beacons from a Celtic clan
The hill of trees, past forest from another time
of charcoal burners or keepers of the consul's vine.

No welcome here, as brambles thick with thorn
Emerge like guards, through brackens tangled form
Tearing the unwary, restraining, bar the way
As wire whipping barbs, grow strong throughout the clay.

Earth's retreating frosts, gouge sleek the treacle ground
Ferns crumble under footholds, each frond a powdered brown
This heavy strides an effort, it's hostile and unkind
These woods can do without us and forces us to mind.

It seems to have no yielding, yet, just beyond our gaze
A flock of sheep, wool matted, huddle quiet to graze
Heads turn to stare, black faced, with large enquiring eyes
This peaceful scene beguiles us, beneath the evening skies.

Tall pines protect this landscape as evidence appears
when cloven hoof and barking, betrays the shy roe deer
Close by the sacred holly, attesting Saturn's might
Tho' berries, red since Autumn, proclaim a Godly light.

Homer

HEAVENLY THOUGHTS

All roads lead to heaven
        whichever one you take.
Select the path of 'bluebells'
        'cowslips' and 'rape'
Avoid the lanes of chaos
        disturbing peace of mind
Seek tranquil countryside
        leave the noise behind

Little plots of heaven
        placed beneath the sky
Flowers in array, meadows,
        known to you and I
Jewelled treasure chest
        rays of golden hue
Diamonds are the daisies
        set in buttercups for you

Earth is our heaven
        enjoy it every day
Appreciate our wildlife
        do not walk away
Convey this to the young ones
        innocence supreme
Allow them the honour
        to live within a dream.

Maureen May Weitman

FORGET ME NOT

What a carpet of blue -
these flowers do give.
A single flower does not -
give much of a display.

But a patch of hundreds,
What a wealth of colour they give.
Reflecting the sky above.
Should one forget the other.

Growing beside a country lane.
Saying to all who pass by.
Please forget me not.
And give the message I give.

Spread it all around -
Far and wide, until -
the whole world takes note.
Do forget me not.

Norman Mason

SEASONS

Spring - is awakening!
        A hue of freshness o'er the earth
        An end to darkness
        The promise of new birth

Summer - is living
        When all our days are long
        Vibrant colours - growing - singing
        Warm earth and sweet birdsong

Autumn - is quietness!
        The earth now settled down
        Changing hues and distant views
        Through countryside and town

Winter - is resting!
        Clear skies - darkness descends
        A suspension of nature
        Reflections - birdsong ends!

Seasons - ever changing
        Rich pattern of our lives
        With all that nature offers
        This England . . . thrives.

Mary S Jones

LEAVE THE WHALES ALONE PLEASE

Leave the whales alone please,
Let them sing their songs,
Leave the whales alone please,
Let them live at ease.

Kayleigh Louise Bowen (10)

THE CAT WITH THE GOLDEN EYES

What wondrous images are there
Within those orbs of liquid gold,
Unfathomable pools of light,
Their depths unknown, their tales untold.

How many centuries ago
Stood thou beside the Pharaoh's throne.
Proud and aloof, no servant thou,
Thy spirit free, thy power unknown.

Could I but gaze into thine eyes,
And see the things which thou hast seen
Throughout the years, then would I be
Enriched with wonders unforeseen.

But thou dost only sit and stare
At things unseen by mortal men,
Lost in thy dreams of long ago,
Of sights and sounds beyond our ken.

Proud cat, who condescends to take
The love I give, my home to share,
When I am sad, and need a friend
To comfort me, then you are there.

Beloved cat, with golden eyes,
Although you sit upon my knee
Content and happy with your lot,
I do not own you - *you* own *me*!

Hilda Brown

OCTOBER DAY

Sky overcast at early dawn,
A chill pervades the air,
Cold droplets threaded on the lawn
A time for grey despair.
Then, fantasy of swirling mist,
Light striving hard to shred
The rising veils of cloud, sun kissed,
Turning from pink to red.
Suddenly! As if on stage,
The gauzy curtains rise.
Sol's entrance now will joy presage
As through the East he flies.
Push back the icy winter days;
Seek summer to recapture.
Reach out to warming, golden rays,
To Indian summer's rapture.
October . . . autumn's prelude write,
Approaching year's final read.
Yet still the future shining bright
Sleeps in the earth in dormant seed.

E Balmain

NATURE

Nature is such a wonderful thing
Just think of the treasures the
             seaside can bring
The golden sand stretching for miles
The splashing of waves, the sea so blue
Children building sandcastles
They look so happy too

Shells all different shapes and colours
Dolphins, seals their eyes so wide
Crabs in rockpools where they like to hide
Penguins in their black and white uniforms

Jellyfish, seaweed that gets in your toes
Where the sea ends no-one knows
Whatever the weather the tide
Still comes and goes

Janis Pearson

SUMMER SNOW

Surprised by the June shower
We sheltered by the hawthorn tree
At the wood's edge.
Around us, in a green arc,
Nettles and Queen Anne's lace
Shuddered in the watery violence.
Yet closer, the heavy drops,
Failing to penetrate the leaves,
Dashed petals from the white blooms -
The warm rain turning to snow.
We stood, in the summer of our love,
And thought of the coming winter.

Jeffrey C Barham

MY SON

I kneel upon the floor,
Place my arm upon the chair.
I look at the child I love,
Laid peacefully, sleeping there.
I feel my joyful heart,
As I've never felt before.
And as the years pass by,
I'll love him more and more.
I lean and gently kiss him,
No movement does he make,
Except the beating of his heart,
The heart I'll never break.
His eyes they slowly open,
He gently smiles at me.
My heart it swells with pride,
This happy sight to see.
He's smooth and he's so tender,
His life has just begun.
I'll always love and cherish him,
My flesh, my blood, my son.

John Millar Kent

NATURE

*(Wisdom and spirit of the universe! Thou soul, that art the
eternity of thought! - Wordsworth, 1799)*

What mean we by this? Not the qualities
Of a person, or thing, or essential
Character, hard, or soft, or generous,
But the whole system, arrangements, forces,
Plants, animals, and virgin scenery.
What are we to make of these as, tired,
We flee our towns and cities harsh, to wend
Towards the mountains rearing high to peaks
So dignified and lofty, far above
Our devious ways. Calm lakes, shimmering,
Speak volumes of charmed insight echoing
Down valleys fervent with music from
Streams becoming rivers flowing over
Waterfalls, silver curtains billowing
To breezes' soft commands. Mystic forests
Speak of history, and the web of time,
Telling us, expectantly, that we can,
If we but wish, refuel at will - even
Though we must - from the Maker's heart, so far,
So close. Enchanted, let us listen to
The silence. Life renews in birth again
To prove nature's law adamant for growth,
If only we co-operate,
Breathing deep, drafts of tonic wine.

Desmond Tarrant

NATURE

Birds and animals everywhere
roaming about on the landscape
peace and quiet, calm and still
they will stay
until someone comes and takes it all away
there they lay all calm and still
because someone had gone out on a hunt
to kill.

Emma-Jane Gray

SNOW STORM

Watching winter
Out of windows
Scatter arms of cold ash out,
Flowing feather flacks
Flocking in side winds,
Wild in each orbit
Go twisting about.

Storming fragility
Blown down ungrounding
Hovers unbidden
To dazzle the spot,
Where my cupidity
Dreaming of might be,
Comes to the vision
My now had forgot.

M Faulkner

FLEDGLING ROBINS

That mon liege with a red breast
Leaves his fledglings to fly the nest
First flutterings of new born wings
Whilst he sits in a tree and sings
A stalk of hay gives rise a tremble
At the nestlings' first preamble
One after another hop around
Bewilderdly upon the ground
Tentatively test their nursery flight
And try again until they get it right
Cock robin encourages them with each trill
And off they fly when acquired their skill

Francis Arthur Rawlinson

LAKEHURST PLACE

Sweet the scent of narcissus
  And daffodils adrift 'neath the trees
Walk the paths of Lakehurst Place
  With a gentle, spring-like breeze!
'Tis a lovely vista before you
  Magnolia trees do abound,
You will stand and stare with wonder
  At the huge pink flowers around!
Rhododendrons in scarlet coats blazing
  As tall as twelve feet I do swear,
Some here are white as the lily
  Adorning a fair maiden's hair!
'Tis the place to go when you are tired
  Of city life, or of the town
Just to sit there in peace and in quiet
  And to simply just let your hair down!
Savour the wonderful colours
  Of the birds that swim on the lake
Sapphire blue, interwoven with emerald
  And all for your eyes' sake!
Without doubt, you'll want to return here,
  To this garden of Eden so sweet,
It's one of the nicest I've been to
  For *me* this day is complete!

Maisie Trussler

FELLOW FRIEND

Lonely gull,
your tireless dance
of earth and sky.
Soft blend of muted
memories from a distant dream.
Dimmed cries of
chorused chimes to
stir the pulse,
and soar to heights
beyond the earth-bound soul.

Scavenger of man.
Hid 'neath the carefree
raptures of your wind-blown
wings, blatant desires
to seize at life.

Lonely gull,
I feel your strength,
and tilt my heart to
brave tempestuous life.
My streamlined beauty,
a mask to hide,
what I devour, destroy.

Eileen Real

Snowdrop

Thou little herald of our dawning year
Kindling thy flame of life at Life's own fire -
The Joy of God is in thy frail form singing,
In thy white bells His Purity and Peace
His Exultation in thy green swords springing
And His unbroken Mercy in thy drooping head.

Sister Rosamund Helen

SUMMER CALM

A summer afternoon and still the air,
As nothing stirs beneath a cloudless sky,
Halcyon days are here again with skies set fair,
A time of fruitfulness, when swifts fly high.

Roses give up their perfume to the bees,
Which hum around the honeysuckle vine,
We listen to the birdsong in the trees,
While savouring the taste of summer wine.

Soon, perhaps, the blue skies will turn grey,
And storms may dash rose petals to the ground,
For now we'll make the most of summer days,
With sunlight, warmth and calmness all around.

Barbara Pearton

HOMELINESS

Pine laden a landscape green,
Breathtaking beauty our pleasant land,
Rugged hills tumbling into dark blue seas,
No ghosts, crowds or legend-only myth.

Lost that feeling of a couch potato,
A warmer sun washes away many tears,
Brief encounters of old and new,
Never strange walking in wonderland.

Curious greens pleasing themselves,
Making everyone believe; are they artistic?
Demanding and taking limelight around,
Well established for all to see.

Nothing sacred when promoting themselves,
Acid or alkaline stint growth none,
Interweaving thoughts pleasing; not always,
Their stress now seen not man-made.

Forgive me if I ramble on,
Beyond any price this part of heaven,
A friend not to politely hollowed,
Plenty of backache there mate.

Jon Aspinall

LABURNUM

The day . . . the memory . . . dust motes dancing
In the sun's rays - bold colours romancing,
Fresh like the Very First Day - unmuted,
Dawning untouched, unmarr'd, unpolluted,
Shining brightly . . .
                    clean, clean . . .
                                    undistorted.

Heat hazy on the open road, the rich smell
Of sweet-mown hay, carried on the wind to dwell
Forever treasur'd, well-remember'd - and more,
Insinuating subtly on mem'ry's store,
Penetrating . . .
                deep, deep . . .
                                your very core.

The road winding, winding to the blue sea, hedg'd
By a terraced hillside at the ocean's edge,
A bank of golden rain growing, there adorning,
Slight fragrant pendulous blooms deeply glowing,
Like a cascade . . .
                    down, down . . .
                                    softly flowing.

Gwendoline Douglas

SORREL-FINGERS (REAP AND SOW)

Out of town where nature dwells
about Sunday-morning's peal of bells
live the folk of countryside
by village clock they sleep and rise . . .

Tilled
black - rugged
sods
of earth
across
bare fields
strewn - frowns of turf
where between
the divots
gently lay
seven seas of corn
come May . . .
Though
springtime green
at rainbow's end
by summer - ripe
gold ears to lend
Come autumn
harvest
milled for bread
the field
sleeps fallow . . .

Man well-fed!

Here - ploughmen lunch at Wheatsheaf Inn
a pint of ale - a chat - a grin
afore the land put back to toil
between the hedgerows' fertile soil . . .

Barry Howard

MORNING

This morning is filled with memories.
Such crisp frost recalls Christmas past.
On a morning like this
Our goat broke into the vegetable patch
And scrunched the frozen tops
Of cabbages intended for the spring.
On such a morning too
Old Fred McGrath was found dead on his path.
He'd slipped on his cottage step, looking
For what the day might bring.
On a morning like this
We all stare into the light for any change
And listen for that murmur in the land
Which signifies the onset of another spring.

Pamela M Henderson

WATER AND RAIN

If I were a painter,
Which regretfully I am not;
I would rush with palette and brush
To capture the moment and the watery scene.

So I must afterwards be a writer,
Albeit second best for the moving song;
And do what is describingly within my power
To convey that which impressed me so strong.

A smooth-flowing river, not quite a flood,
Grey brown, sullied by mud
Was under me on the bridge where I stood;
Along the path wandering to the town.

Returning the same way but in the wet,
The river surface was now dented by rain,
Just like a reversed seasoning pepper pot;
A moving colander of perforated splashing effect.

Eric Ashwell

AN ENCHANTED PLACE

Out of all the wonders of nature the rainbow is the best.
Through claps of thunder and bursts of sun the rainbow stands the test.
So beautiful and delicate arched in majesty
The colours of pastel are plain for all to see.
And then in contrast an electric storm in a flash
Cuts across ebony skies like an ugly gash.
Rain that follows penetrates the earth in a mighty rage
Sheeting down and trapping all within its cage.
The calm after the storm is silent and sweet
Where the forces of nature decide to meet.
The storm passes by leaving clouds to unfold
And the magic of the rainbow with its pot of gold.

Gena McCrystal

HEDGE FLOWERS OF PEMBROKESHIRE

Tall trees leaned their great branches above us,
weaving deep green leafy tunnels, from which
we emerged, to sunshine and bright hedges.
Clear green blades of swaying vernal grasses,
grew high, with their own intrinsic beauty
enhanced, by the mingling of wild flowers.
Proudly soaring in their midst, moon daisies,
their rays, light shining, purest white and chaste.
Near the roads' verges, ruby red clovers,
buttercups, radiant with sunlit gloss,
pincushion clumps of tiny bird's-foot trefoil,
scarcely noticeable, so lowly born,
red campions, cock robins of the hedgerow,
slender-stemmed white stichwort. Many hedges
adorned with profusions of Queen Anne's lace,
a network of clustered exuberance.
Standing high, against rocks and woody shrubs,
some appearing 'mid fronds of sturdy ferns,
stately foxgloves, conspicuous, handsome,
with inflorescence of rich, purple bells,
leaves, proud possessor of curative drug.
The hills were ablaze with brave, golden gorse,
spine protected against animals and water loss.
The hedges dipped down to grey stone walls,
pink valerian clinging to crevices.
Beyond the walls grew Welsh yellow poppies,
fragile, small and delicate as windflowers.
Wild flowers, nature's precious gift to us.
Their joy in being allowed to grow unchecked,
freedom for their own floral arrangements,
infinite variety unchallenged,
assurance of wild, ecstatic beauty.

Iris Jones

HUMAN AGAINST NATURE

Can you remember the times, perhaps recall, when at school,
it was common-place seeing things, then, like frogs in a pool?
Tadpoles, small fishes - all were there for us to see.
Catch one, and this made us shout out with glee!
Nature walks taught us of, the beauty all around,
from the birds in their nests, to the flowers upon the ground.
Where quite common to eye, one saw, bluebell, buttercup -
sadly now though, mostly gone, through being killed off - dug up.
That occurrence has stemmed through what's called progress,

in the main -
seeing the many once places of beauty decimated - it does

seem a shame.
And for what . . . ? A new road perhaps - or building, in place -
many coming forth to hide, what these areas once graced.
And in my years to come, perhaps, the asking might be of me.
'Can you tell me at all, what once around here was like what one

could see?'
Then with pride of remembering - how it was; as it had been,
I shall recall times of frogs, bluebells, buttercups . . . and all of
the other things that I had seen!

Brian Cartwright

BEACH AUTUMN

The wind-blown sand moves like snakes.
Becomes hills and hollows, like small earthquakes.
The sky is high, and bright clear blue.
The sun, gives a beautiful golden hue.
Above, white clouds skirt to and fro.
Below, waves capped like promised snow.
A beach in autumn lets you see.
Nature's changing majesty.

Sheila Mack

THE KITE'S RETURN

My mind's excited - with what thrill
To watch the kites from Christmas Hill.
Sweeping above the frosted trees
Loose-winged, soaring with graceful ease.

And even through the frozen squall
The dance continues, with shrill call
Across the valley, circling still
From steep pasture to gorsey hill.

With flick of tail they alter course
Hanging above the wild wind's force.
Hackles of grey and bright yellow eyes,
Fork-tailed masters of the skies.

But while I watch this rare display
My heart is filled with deep dismay,
For I belong to the very race
That tried such beauty to efface.

Marilyn Lowe

A WALK IN THE WOODS

If you walk in the woods on a bright spring day
You will see masses of bluebells, a lovely display.
Wild violets and primroses you will also see there
And lots of wild garlic will be scenting the air.

But one must tread softly so as not to disturb
The mating and nesting of all the wild birds.

If you walk through the woods on a hot summer day
The trees will protect you from the sun's fierce ray.
But look out for the wildlife roaming around,
You may see deer or foxes and rabbits abound.
Many eyes will be watching you to see what you do,
From the wise old owl to the pointed-nose shrew.

If you walk through the woods on a dry autumn day
You might see the grey squirrel storing its nuts away.
There should be lots of wild fungi for you to see.
But you must not pick them unless you know what they be.
The colours of autumn are a sight to be seen,
The gold and the red taking place of the green.

If you walk through the woods on a cold winter's day
You won't see the squirrel it will be snug in its drey.
The fox will be sheltering safe in its den,
Away from the sound of foxhunting men.
There should be plenty of berries on the old holly tree.
Wherever you walk there is always something to see.

Phyllis Ing

Nature's Way

Have you watched a flock of birds soar across the sky
and marvelled at their instinct as they go flying by
Have you watched a new-born lamb struggle to its feet
and skip towards its mother to give a happy bleat

Have you watched the springtime buds slowly start to bloom
and give your garden colour after winter's gloom
Have you watched a mountain stream become a waterfall
and enrich the land around it where trees grow straight and tall

Have you watched a waterlily open in the morning sun
and slowly close to go to sleep when the day is done
Have you watched a rainbow fade away from view
and wondered at the colours that make up its varied hue

Have you watched the trees cut down so Man can build a road
Have you watched the tankers spill their oily load
Have you watched the wildlife disappear and die
Have you ever stopped to ask yourselves the question, 'Why?'

Helen E Urquhart

NATURE'S WORLD

In the spring.
You have to sing.
Having fun.
Can be done.

In the summer.
I feel younger.
Running around.
On the ground.

In the autumn.
People courting.
Rustling sound.
Of leaves on the ground.

In the winter.
I feel like a sprinter.
Darting from place to place.
Icy cold winds on my face.

Carpet of green.
Covered in clover.
One of the signs to be seen.
That nature's taken over.

Jason High (14)

IT'S A WONDERFUL, WONDERFUL WORLD

Dreams of fancy, dancing in the air, like Tinkerbell
Volcanic flames burning underground as if from hell
Crashing waves, pounding on the shores in heavy seas
Raging wind, speeding all the clouds, or gentle breeze
Wild horses galloping across the moors with clattering hooves
Country cottages, rambling roses round the door and thatched roofs

Butterflies all landing on the flowers, with coloured wings
A blackbird at the early break of dawn, oh how it sings
Poppy fields, mountain peaks, and rivers flowing on
Meadows, buttercups and daisies, baby ducklings on a pond
Apples, acorns, chestnuts, dropping from a tree
Wondrous nature, for those who really look, and then they see

The whirring sound of flying swans on high
Yellow chicks, woolly lambs, a new-born baby hear its cry
Found under gooseberry bush, or delivered by a stork?
Raindrops pitter-patter, hail and waterfalls - listen to their talk
The scent of evening primrose, fresh-cut grass or crimson rose
White fluffy snowflakes, just like cotton wool before they froze

Salmon leaping up a Scottish river, soon to spawn
Wake up just as the sun is rising, see the dawn
Changing years from dinosaurs to rocket ships and soon
In 1969 man first walked upon the moon
Jet black skies with fairy lights of twinkling stars
Perhaps one day - a very bold adventure - to Planet Mars

Man will be man - to join the eternal race
To conquer jungles, Arctic poles, and space
And unravel mysteries yet unfurled
But we already have a wonderful world
Why? The answer is 'because it's there' . . . it seems
Just another part of our fanciful dreams

Freda Baxter

THE ROPE OF TIME

The rope of time slips through one's hands,
Each knot a passing day.
We little heed its progress as
It travels on its way.
When the days seem all too short
The rope skips nimbly by,
And when they seem to have no end
It lingers like a sigh.
Seasons come and seasons go,
Nature's changing face,
The rope of time meticulously
Keeping silent pace.
Busy with our daily lives
We let ourselves pretend
Our rope will keep on sliding by,
Forever, without end.

Frank Jensen

THE SEA SHORE

Oh! Sea of wrath, Oh! Sea of storm
How calm you look this summer morn
Gentle waves lapping the beach
Almost within my fingers' reach
What lies within your mysterious deeps?
Little shells and sharks and reefs
Sunken wrecks; gold or pearls
Maybe even mermaid girls!
Whales and turtles, hidden caves
All these things and more
Lie beneath your reckless waves
Which now are gently breaking on the shore.

Joan King

COLD, COLD WINTER

Winter is here, and the long hot summer has gone
It was like yesterday, on the porch as the sun shone
Warm and comfortable, drinking home-made beer
Writing cards to friends, wishing they were all here

In summer, even when hot, there seems lots to be done
Yet in winter, everything is cold, only children have fun
There is no sunbathing, ice-cream, or games on the beach
Only keeping warm, and clearing snow away out of reach

The gardens look shabby, with the grass thin and well worn
Trees have shed their last leaves, looking bare and so forlorn
Snow lies all around, on houses, on footpaths, and on roads
While machines do their best clearing it away in lorry loads

Some people have lots of fun, when winter comes around
Ice-skating, sleigh rides, making snowmen on the ground
It is cold, very cold, with ice on the roads and the houses
Thick woollen jumpers, overcoats, and no more thin blouses

This is just the beginning, and will get worse in time, I swear
For most animals have the right idea, they hibernate each year
We human beings, must take what Mother Nature may send
No matter how cold, we grin and bear it to the bitter end

Christmas comes and still very cold, then comes early spring
For a few hours the sun shows itself, giving life a new meaning
And as the days go by, the sun gets warmer and shines more
Suddenly winter has gone, no more cold only sunshine galore

William A Laws

LET THE COUNTRYSIDE BE MY HOME

A life of fun is all I ask,
No master to implore a task,
Only time that is free to roam,
The open countryside my home,

Make my bed upon a hill top,
And through the night sleep bare
And stop,
Awake to birds singing in tree,
With a feeling of being free,

For breakfast an apple or two,
And apple with fresh water chew,
Afterwards putting on my shoe,
And going off to somewhere new.

Novello N Maynard-Thompson

DURDLE DOOR

The cry of the gulls lifts my spirits skyward,
Amongst them I embrace the wind.
Painting threads of freedom across the blue canvas sky
Above boat speckled sea.

Cupped by rugged cliff and sleepy sands
Of heavy heart, I am no more.
To nourish the soul and enrich my mind
The teasing waves beckon,
Whispering shells, and salt steeped pebbles.

At one with the sea ghosts I travel the tides,
On the breath of sails, to the frothy rockpools.
Bathed in seaspray on rock-a-bye decks
I wake from slumber, once more to shore

Amidst clouds, inhaled. On craggy, sun-toasted summit.
I shall return to take my fill.

Diane Jean Wood

COMPANIONS FOR LIFE

Faithful energetic sporting dogs of the world
Maybe my message can now be unfurled
Huskies, English bull terrier, sheepdog, Labrador
All have and many more their part to play
Some deserve medals at the end of the day
The huskies travel for miles on tracks of hard packed snow
Loyal to their masters determined to please and instinct which
we all know

Master and dogs able to arrive at an
Appointed place with temperatures below
Many hazards on the way
Pleased I think at the end of the day
English bull terriers a dog so true to a family
Noble in stature one could easily become proud
Seen at major dog shows, sweeps the board
When others are around
A trained and well-behaved pet is a
Compliment in all spheres
One could say here here
The English sheepdog is from the legends of the past
Still the farmer's favourite his sheep would soon become lost.
Such intelligence to gently drive them
Away from crags, crevices, waterfalls
And other dangers to the fold
A wonder of nature to behold
Sheepdog trials their masterfulness is displayed
In their ability to do the job that is required
When it comes to the end of their working life
Some live with the family a pet cared for no strife

The Labrador a wonderful dog I cannot say more
Whose shiny coat and clear eyes
Show they are well-loved which is no surprise
The tremendous aid he gives to a blind man
His sight and dedication not to mention the
Rapport between the dog and the owner
Seen together in the streets and you will
Soon discover
The wonderful power of Mother Nature
That no other force can meet
Such a feat.

Mabel E Nickholds

OPTIMISM DURING A TIME OF WAITING
(To Sue)

Today, as reticent summer must have been
Sulking somewhere
Behind the rolls of grey May cloud,
Behind the boisterous wind, butting the wrestling,
Whipping treetops,
The crisp heather on the fresh Chase wheezed
And the numb random stones stood stock
And the hollow hill hunched
And the dark birds skated on air,
Waiting for the richness of the sunlight.

We knew their summer would come.
And ours.

David J Ayres

THE FROST

The frost on the grass,
Casts a blanket of white,
That falls to the ground,
As we sleep in the night,
Changing the look,
Of the earth that we know,
To a sparkling white vista,
Reminiscent of snow,
The trees and the shrubs,
Have that frosty white look,
While ice starts to form,
On the slow moving brook,
Steam forms a cloud,
On our breath as we talk,
The nip in the air,
Reddens cheeks as we walk,
But these are the things,
At this time of the year,
We come to expect,
Now that winter is near.

Andrew Quinn

THE COUNTRY

The thing about the country
with sights and sounds and smell.
If you've got your wits about you
what's gone before you, you can tell.

When the rabbits are out feeding,
then all around is calm.
But if the bunnies have gone missing
man or beast has caused alarm.

You'll maybe see a bird of prey
hovering overhead,
Or catch a foxy scent -
perhaps a human form instead.

The nightjars and their chattering
are a lovely sound at dusk.
To hear nightingales sing,
for me is just a must.

When the rain has fallen
if roe and fallow are around,
You can see where they've been hiding
they leave their 'slots' in muddy ground.

Undergrowth is flattened
into comfy private beds.
Bark rubbed off under branches,
as they scratch their itching heads.

These things are so rewarding
if the countryside you like.
So slow down and enjoy it
leave the car and take a hike.

Lesley Smith

THE HEAVENLY NATURE

Walking through the woodland amid the greenery,
Swaying graciously,
Are trees in all their glory
Some very tall, many small
Reminding me of Nature's Cathedral.
Far beyond lies the deep blue sea
Here in the woods for you, as well as me,
Such lovely things to see.
The butterflies, are they not beautiful things?
Many adorned with gloriously coloured wings.
There are numerous shapes and sizes
Flitting from flower to flower
Sometimes folded nestling in sweet scented bowers.
Often in the honeysuckle, chasing with the bees
Merrily fluttering round and round
Such pretty things to see.
I've often wished that I had wings like these,
To mingle in the lilac trees
And to fly in the gentle breeze.
Oh! For wings like a dove, to fly above
Betwixt the starlights,
And try to reach the 'Heavenly Heights';
There to abide in everlasting joy,
And perfect peace.

Madeline Green

COLOURS

Colours make us feel happy, or sad,
Making life worth living, and feeling glad,

Gone is the grey, of winter's gloom.
Soon . . . all the flowers, are in full bloom.

Red, yellow, green, and purple,
Rush to see the flowers hurtle,

Along the borders, they huddle round
Pushing hard for life, beneath the ground,

Tall and small their colours blaze,
Where beauty is a constant maze,

Perfumes waft, on a summer breeze,
Drifting up, to dreaming trees.

The sun shines through a summer shower,
Bringing sweet relief, to thirsty flowers.

A rainbow high above us all,
Throws colours across, a garden wall.

Saffron soft, to the hue of the sky,
Bring peace and tranquillity to the heart, from the eye!

Sylvia Connor

THE MOVING CLOUDS

I have watched the clouds go slowly by,
Across a sky of blue,
And I oft'times wonder, why and where,
Those clouds, are going to.

I have seen them unfold a mantle of
gloom,
And they seem to say, what fun,
To curtain the sky, in the heavens
above,
And blot out, the moon and the sun.

While the clouds will move from place
to place,
On prevailing winds that blow,
And in the seasons of the year,
Will deliver, rain, sleet and snow.

Clouds will sometimes disappear,
And leave a clear blue sky,
To give glorious sunshine all
day long,
And starry skies at night.

But clouds will come and clouds will
go,
To be floating around forever,
And help those folk who like to
think,
They can really, forecast the weather.

John H Hill

THE BUTTERFLY

Gentle creature fair and bright
Settling on my hand so light,
Your wings a gossamer thread
With gold and brown and orange spread,
Whose creation fills our mind
The wonder of your beauty find.
It is here, for just a minute seen
Look well, enjoy and ever dream.

Betty Samson

SUNSET

As the sun sinks slowly in the west.
Heaven is telling earth it is time to rest.
Birds and bees and even flowers
Welcome the coolness of night-time hours.

But if on my bed I sleepless lie
The night-time hours go slowly by.
Lord spread Thy presence round my bed.
Calm my ferverish fears and dread
Of a future unknown.

When evening comes, a man comes home from his daily toil,
Working in the fields, turning the soil.
At the end of the day he has given of his best
Now home calls, for a nice hot meal -
And a good night's rest.

D Turner

SOMEONE
(Inspired by Sister Mercy)

Someone who loves you
Someone who cares
Someone who you know
Will always be there
Someone who will pick you up
When you fall
Someone who will hear you
Whenever you call
Someone who will lift you
When you feel blue
Someone who walks with you
Every day of your life
Someone who will be with you
In times of strife
Someone who was with you
At the start of your life
Someone who will be with you
At the end of this life
Someone who will guide
To a new life above
And welcome you with pure spirit love

Joan Fowler

MY FLOWER DAYS

I love these flower-filled days,
Each wondrous day more fair,
With aching body, yet filled with love
And the sun-kissed soil in my tangled hair.

Lost in earth's never-ending creation,
Entwined in bird song, the beauty of each flower,
The never-failing love of *God* I see,
So there I go my way, take my fill
Hour by hour.

Florence Andrews

HEAVEN'S DELIGHT

Cumulus wispy white, you be part of the heaven's delight.
Flying higher than any man-made kite, hovering mid-air
your mode of flight.
Never stopping to take a rest, you drift along where the
wind knows best, sometimes East, sometimes West.
Far must you carry your vital load, gathering moisture
as you float along.
Drifting far across the seas and way beyond our open roads,
someday soon you will sing your song.
Amidst lightning's flash and thunder's roar, through the
air you still soar.
Until opening up your heart, one day the rains do pour.
Through your very being the sun does shine, while far
below on picnic we may dine.
You be always there, whether it be night or day,
delivering your gift of life as you travel along the
heavenly highway.
With never a thought of what you may gain, to cover the
world is your aim.
Bringing forth that gift of God's life-giving rain.

Phil Dee

JACK FROST

He's been around with his brush again,
In the still of the cold winter night.
He's painted a magical wonderland,
And clothed all the earth in white.

Like the filigree lace, is the spider's web,
As it clings, to the garden wall.
The trees are all covered, in pearly white,
Like a beautiful white lace shawl.

The dangling twists of the icicles,
Hang like barley sugar strands,
The glinting and glistening of the rime,
As it shines like diamanté fronds.

He crept along in the dead of night,
To create this wonderful sight,
Of a magical winter wonderland,
Of the earth all covered in white.

E M Dolphin

DOING WHAT COMES NATURALLY

The day was smiling on us all
As clouds were fluffy white
Progressing slowly through the sky
Of blue - a pretty sight.

Brightly shone the sun that day -
I shared the smiles around
As folk sauntered in the park
On nature's bright green ground.

A night of stormy weather
Gave me thoughts of doom and gloom.
The thunder roared its anger
'til the dawn's light lit my room.

The morning smelt so fresh and clean -
I did not need a fan.
The shrubs and flowers proudly stood -
They'd drunk life's watering can.

England's green and pleasant lands
Know nature's changing moods
That help or hinder a farmer's world
As he grows all kinds of foods.

Springtime and the summer
Autumn - wintertime.
Seasons of fruitfulness
All fall into line.

Mother Nature is in control -
She mostly brings much order.
I feel it is us who interfere
Here and across the nation's border.

Pat Melbourn

MEMORIES

Can you recall the beauty, of a world
that used to be? When trees and fields
of lovely buttercups, were there to
pick all free!

A time for all the bluebells, the daisies
and the sun; the meadows, and the flowing
stream; a place where we had fun!

A tree to climb, then to swing from;
its branches O! So strong, then to
fall among those soft brown leaves,
then laugh with happy song.

A changing world we've come to;
you can't go here or there;
everything is private; and buildings
now stand there. Never mind!

We have our memories, but the
children of today. They play in
all those buildings; where we
were young. We say!

E Sharpley

NATURE'S WAY

So serene and calm am I,
at peace with all around.
Day into night. Time goes by,
I barely whisper a sound.
Then.
Something stirs, way up there,
chanting, teasing, dare, dare, dare.
Evoked in me a mighty rage,
Hatred. I shall lash out hard,
a fear you cannot cage.
Look
I will join forces, and how,
you shall run and cower now.
I shall rise above the land,
and you shall feel my mighty hand.
And.
Beating down upon the ground,
only a path of destruction
to be found.
Battle on, some more shall I,
and you shall ask, how and why.
When.
Until the time, as before,
Nature's allies, shall part once more.
When I am gone, and you can mourn,
The passing of a mighty storm.

Tania Varndell

TURNAROUND

Turnaround upon white winter hill.
All is quiet and very still.
Sky and hill merge into one,
Mine alone to walk upon.
Turnaround upon the hill in spring,
Look forward to sweet scents it brings.
Shades of green and palest blue,
Each new day a different hue.
Turnaround as summer takes its hold,
Colours on the hill are bold,
Summer sky's pure shimmering gold.
Turnaround as autumn mists unfold,
Fallen leaves a carpet make,
Winter follows once more in its wake.
All nature's seasons now have turned,
Eternal in their turning.

Christine Beebee

CLOUD-RAPT

A moorland garden swathed in clinging cloud.
A saturated mist, a vapour shroud
That drapes familiar bushes, ferns and trees,
And hides all but the nearest sight of these.

I walk a step or two, and would be lost
Were not the lawn my own and often crossed,
Though now the grass is pale with droplets fogging,
And at the edge, where fallen leaves lie sogging,
A slug slides in his heaven of decay,
Digesting what the trees have thrown away.

All berries wear a drop of clear confection,
A crystal bauble formed in round perfection,
Till one becomes a silent tear, and falls
On ivy darkly hugging to the walls.
Nearby the leafless branches wetly weep
On blanket soil wherein the snowdrops sleep.

A gentle breath disturbs the veil a trace,
To tantalise my eyes with swelling space,
But, flowing back again, I am once more
Enveloped in opaqueness as before.

There is no sun, no ray of warming light,
No rain, no gale, no snow or freezing bite.
Only November's mantle, moistly grey,
Enwraps my world in nature's balm today.

Patricia Farley

WELCOME TO AUTUMN

Once again the fields are bare,
The corn's stored away, there's a nip in the air,
Blackberries hang on the wayside bramble,
Children return to school with a scramble.

The summer's been lovely, now it is past,
We're back to autumn's long evenings at last,
It is always the same as seasons slip by,
'Oh, summer has gone' we say with a sigh.

Hedgerows are gay with berries bright,
The autumn sun has set alight,
Wild rosehips are shiny and red,
Ruddy haws nestle in their thorny bed.

Our feathered friends enjoy the tasty fare,
They know winter will soon be here,
Trees and hedges will all be bare,
No more food for them to share.

Who would forego the lovely sight,
Of a misty morning or the harvest moonlight,
For autumn is winter's gentle guide,
Who leads us from summer to happy Christmastide.

Margery English

INFORMATION

We hope you have enjoyed reading this book - and that you will continue to enjoy it in the coming years.

If you like reading and writing poetry drop us a line, or give us a call, and we'll send you a free information pack.

Write to :-
**Anchor Books Information
1-2 Wainman Road
Woodston
Peterborough
PE2 7BU
(01733) 230761**